The Artist's Palate

  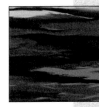  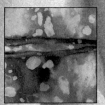

recipes and artwork from
members and friends of the
marblehead arts association

Credit: Suzanne Naudin

www.marbleheadarts.org

Credit: Herb Goldberg

The Artist's Palate
Copyright ©2017 by the Marblehead Arts Association
ISBN-10: 1547026650
ISBN-13: 978-1547026654

Requests for information or additional book orders should be addressed to:

Marblehead Arts Association
The Hooper Mansion, 8 Hooper Street, Marblehead, MA 01945
Telephone: 781.631.2608 | www.marbleheadarts.org

Cover image–wonderful paint-dipped wooden spoons as found on:
maisyandgrace.com

Book design by Raven Creative, Inc.
raven2.com | ravencreative.viewbook.com

Marblehead
Arts Association

Now in its 10th decade, the Marblehead Arts Association (MAA) is located in the historic King Hooper Mansion. The MAA was founded in 1922 by a small group of artists who took action to support their beliefs that a vibrant art community was integral to the well-being of Marblehead and the surrounding community. In 1938, the members purchased the dilapidated King Hooper Mansion. Committed to preserving an important piece of Marblehead's history the mansion was restored and in 1975 was admitted to the National Register of Historic Places. This gracious home serves us today, into the twenty-first century, as a superb reminder of the past and the 18th century.

The MAA continues to grow and prosper, currently serving 500+ artistically diverse artist, associate and corporate members. Six galleries of exhibits by association members and guest artists rotate approximately every six weeks displaying over 1,200 original works of art annually. Admission to the galleries is free and open to the public. The mansion is available to rent for corporate events, private parties and weddings.

The Marblehead Arts Association is an integral part of Marblehead and Boston's North Shore, and attracts visitors locally, regionally and internationally. A cornerstone of the MAA is arts education and programming, including classes in all mediums, artist demonstrations, performances and lectures.

We continue to pursue our mission of:

"Leading the arts in the community…
Inspiring generations."

Contents

"My doctor told me I had to stop throwing intimate dinners for four unless there are three other people."

~Orson Welles

Appetizers

"Avocados" by Claudia Kaufman

Avocado & Tomato Aspic

Ingredients

For Aspic:
2 envelopes Knox gelatin
1 teaspoon sugar
1-1/2 cups + 2 cups V8 juice
Dash of Worcestershire sauce
Dash of lemon juice
Salt and pepper

For Filling:
3 ripe avocados
2 tablespoons sour cream
2 tablespoons mayonnaise
1 tablespoon finely chopped onion
2 tablespoons lemon juice
A few drops of green food coloring

Directions

1. Stir gelatin, sugar and the 1-1/2 cups V8 juice over moderate heat until dissolved, about 3 - 4 minutes.
2. Add remaining juice, lemon juice, Worcestershire sauce – salt and pepper to taste.
3. Pour 1/3 cup of aspic into each of 6 - 8 tall sherbet glasses.
4. Chill until firm, about half an hour – keep the rest of the aspic at room temperature.
5. Mash the avocado with other filling ingredients. Add just a few drops of green food coloring until you get a color you like.
6. Spread over each of the sherbets, saving a little to put a dab on the top. Top with remaining aspic and top with a little dab of filling. Chill.

Tips

- This makes a great appetizer at Christmas.
- Adding about 1/4 of a cup of aspic to the top of the filling works well; you can always add more.
- The aspic will be plenty for 8, but you might need an extra avocado if they are small.
- Use the dark bumpy avocados – they are much tastier than the smooth ones.
- This can be made a day or 2 in advance.

Recipe provided by Judy Jacobi

"Garden Greens" by Charlie Allen

Baked Spinach Artichoke Dip

Ingredients

1 cup mayonnaise
1 cup freshly grated parmesan
14 oz. can artichoke hearts
1 package frozen chopped spinach, thawed and squeezed
1/2 cup chopped red pepper
1/4 cup shredded Monterey Jack or mozzarella cheese
Toaster baguette slices, pita chips or crackers

Directions

1. Set oven to 350 degrees.
2. Mix mayonnaise and parmesan.
3. Add artichoke, spinach and bell pepper.
4. Put in 1 quart pie-type dish, cover with Monterey Jack or mozzarella.
5. Cover and bake 15 - 20 minutes until cheese is melted.

Tip

• Makes 24 servings (2 tablespoons each).

Recipe provided by Ann Welch

"People who love to eat are always the best people." ~Julia Child

"Koi" by Elaine Abrams

Caviar Pie

Ingredients
8 hardboiled eggs – separate yolks and whites, chop
1-1/2 cup scallions – white and light green parts
1/4 cup mayonnaise
8 oz. cream cheese, room temperature
8 oz. sour cream
4 - 5 jars of caviar (the Romanoff kind in small jars)

Directions
1. Open the jars of caviar and put it all in a tiny meshed colander. Rinse thoroughly - don't be surprised to see all the dye running from the eggs, it's what they do. Let them dry completely – this can take several hours.
2. Lightly coat small spring form pan with cooking spray.
3. Chop egg whites and combine with mayonnaise until sticky. Spread on the bottom of the spring form pan.
4. Chop green onions and layer on top of the egg whites.
5. Spread crumbled yolks over the onions.
6. Beat cream cheese and sour cream together until smooth. Spread the cream cheese/sour cream mixture on top. The easiest method is to drop in small blobs close together and then spread.
7. Place pan on plate with layer of paper towels between pan and plate and refrigerate at least 3 hours and as much as 24 hours.
8. After chilled, top with the caviar.

Tip
• Serve with bagel chips, water crackers or thinly sliced toast points.

Recipe provided by Missy Fisher
This is a great crowd pleaser and I get so many requests for this recipe.
It can take a little effort, but your guests will love it. Enjoy!

"Mushrooms" by Elaine Abrams

Cheese-Stuffed Mushrooms

Ingredients

8 oz. medium fresh mushrooms (about 18 - 20)
6 slices of bacon
1 small onion (finely chopped)
3 tablespoons mayonnaise
1/2 cup shredded white cheddar cheese

Directions

1. Wash and drain mushrooms; remove stems. Finely chop stems.
2. In medium skillet, cook bacon until crisp. Remove bacon; drain on paper towel. Crumble bacon and set aside. Discard all but 2 tablespoons of drippings from skillet.
3. Sauté mushroom stems and onion in bacon drippings for 3 minutes or until tender; drain thoroughly.
4. In a small bowl, blend bacon, mushroom stems, onion, mayo, and cheese.
5. Fill mushroom caps with stuffing mixture.
6. Place mushrooms filled side-up on ungreased 15 x 10" jelly roll pan. Bake in 350 degree oven for 15 - 20 minutes, or until filling is hot and cheese melted.

Recipe provided by Karen McMahon

"You don't need a silver fork to eat good food."
~Paul Prudhomme

"Crab" by Diane Bragdon

Crab Appetizers with Sweet & Sour Dipping Sauce

Appetizer Ingredients

2 teaspoons Worcestershire sauce

8 oz. cream cheese

6 oz. can crabmeat, drained and flaked
 or buy from the seafood department
 to get some nice chunks

2 green onions with tops, thinly sliced

1/2 teaspoon lemon juice

48 wonton wrappers

Salt to taste

Dipping Sauce Ingredients

1/2 cup rice vinegar

1/2 cup brown sugar

1/2 cup water + 1 tablespoon water

2 teaspoons chili sauce

1/2 cup crushed pineapple, well drained

1 tablespoon cornstarch

Appetizer Directions

1. Preheat oven to 425 degrees. Lightly spray cupcake tins with cooking spray.
2. Combine cream cheese, crab, green onions and Worcestershire sauce.
3. Place 2 wontons in each muffin cup to line.
4. Place 1 tablespoon of filling onto the center of each cup. Moisten the edges with water and fold the wonton skin diagonally to form a pocket, pressing edges to seal.
5. Bake in the preheated oven until golden brown, 12 - 15 minutes.
6. Sprinkle lightly with salt when hot out of the oven.

Dipping Sauce Directions

1. Combine vinegar, brown sugar, water and chili sauce in saucepan over medium heat, whisking to dissolve sugar.
2. Combine cornstarch and 1 tablespoon water in a separate bowl and whisk.
3. Whisk cornstarch mixture into the saucepan and bring to a boil. It should thicken slightly.
4. Let cool, then stir in crushed pineapple.
5. Serve with your Crab Appetizers - Delish!

Recipe provided by Diane Bragdon

"Pre-Guacamole" by Frank Costantino

Guacamole

Ingredients

3 tablespoons chopped onion
1/2 teaspoon minced Serrano chili, or more, to taste
1-1/2 teaspoons finely chopped cilantro leaves
1/2 teaspoon salt, or more, to taste
1 small vine-ripened tomato
2 ripe Hass avocados
Juice from one lemon or lime
Tortilla chips for serving

Directions

1. In a small bowl or traditional mortar, pound the onion, chili and cilantro into a coarse paste.
2. Cut the tomato in half and remove the seeds and juice. Chop the pulp finely and add to the paste.
3. Cut the avocados in half, remove the pit and scoop the pulp into the bowl. Mash the avocado evenly into the pepper/onion mixture.
4. Add the juice of one lemon or lime.
5. Salt to taste and serve with tortilla chips.

Recipe provided by Amy Hourihan

"There is no sincerer love than the love of food."
~George Bernard Shaw

"Allium" by Paul McMahon

Herbed Cheese Balls

Ingredients

2 large bunches fresh basil
2 large bunches fresh thyme
2 large bunches fresh parsley
Sea salt, to taste
(2) 24 oz. containers of full fat plain yogurt (not Greek)

Directions

1. Prepare herb mixture days in advance. While herbs are fresh, separate leaves and discard stems. Let herb leaves air dry for a few days (or scatter on a baking sheet and dry in the oven on low heat, between 100 and 170 degrees – however low your oven will go – for as long as it takes them to dry).
2. Once dry, pulverize the leaves with your fingers, then push all through a fine sieve to remove any remaining stem pieces. Add salt to taste and mix. Store in an airtight jar.
3. To make the cheese balls: Place cheesecloth in a strainer over the sink. Put all the yogurt into the cloth, let sit to drain for 1-1/2 2 hours.
4. Remove yogurt from strainer and wrap in unbleached paper towels; place on 3 stacked paper plates and place in refrigerator overnight (towels and paper plates will soak up more moisture).
5. The next day, remove yogurt from refrigerator and wrap in new unbleached paper towels. Gently squeeze to remove any remaining moisture.
6. Separate yogurt into lumps the size of small meatballs and form into spheres (will make about 12).
7. Scatter some herb mix on a flat surface. Roll each cheese ball in herb mix until covered.

Tips

• Tools and materials you will need include: cheesecloth, a strainer, unbleached natural paper towels and 3 paper plates.
• You will have more herb mixture than you need; it will last quite a while in an airtight jar and can be used for other dishes.
• Serve with a baguette or your favorite crackers; nice if paired with a local honey for drizzle.

Recipe provided by Marianne Murphy

"Italy Imagined" by Eleanor Fisher

Pesto Paradise

Ingredients
(2) 6 oz. cans pitted extra-large black olives
1 cup grated parmesan cheese
1 cup extra virgin olive oil
1 cup dry-roasted, salted macadamia nuts
1 teaspoon of chopped garlic (to taste)
1/2 teaspoon hot pepper flakes (to taste)

Directions
1. Drain liquid from olives and blend all ingredients in food processor until almost smooth, about 1 minute.

Tips
May be used in a variety of ways:
• On crackers or bread.
• Mix in pasta.
• Spread on any meat, fish or chicken before or after cooking.
• Freezes wonderfully.

Recipe provided by Eleanor Fisher

"Age and glasses of wine should never be counted." ~Unknown

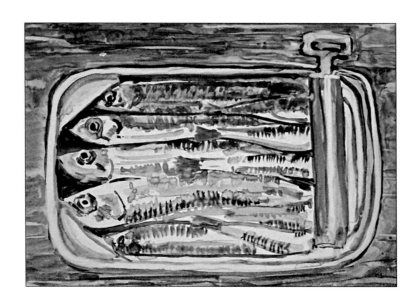

"Sardines" by Amy Hourihan

Warm Sardine & Wilted Spinach Bruschetta

Ingredients

For each sandwich:

2 tablespoons olive oil

2 oz. of fresh, washed spinach

1/2 can of good quality sardines, packed in oil

1 teaspoon dijon mustard

2 slices of toasted and buttered french bread

1 slice of fresh garden tomato

1 wedge lemon

Directions

1. Heat olive oil in a pan over medium heat until it shimmers.
2. Wilt damp spinach in the olive oil, tossing in hot oil, then remove from pan and keep warm.
3. Spread mustard on a slice of the toast.
4. Place warm, wilted spinach over mustard, and then layer this with sardines.
5. Add a thin slice of tomato to top.
6. Squeeze lemon juice over the sandwich and cover with the 2nd piece of buttered toast.

Recipe provided by Amy Hourihan

"It's difficult to think anything but pleasant thoughts while eating a homegrown tomato."

~Lewis Grizzard

"The secret of success in life is to eat what you like and let the food fight it out inside."

~Mark Twain

Sauces, Salads & Dressings

"Cry Babies" by Claudia Kaufman

Grandmere's Salad Dressing

Ingredients

3/4 cup tarragon vinegar
1 tablespoon salt
1-1/2 tablespoons dijon mustard
1 large onion, cut into chunks
1-1/2 teaspoons dried basil
3 garlic cloves
2 stalks celery, including leaves, cut into slices
3 - 4 tablespoons fresh parsley
1-1/2 teaspoons curry powder
1/2 teaspoon dried anise
3 cups canola oil

Directions

1. Puree first 9 ingredients in a blender.
2. Add the oil, along with the anise, slowly through the opening in the lid and blend until smooth.
3. Refrigerate and use for your pleasure.

Recipe provided by Judy Jacobi

My parents were friends of Grandmere Graeter, a French woman who was a fabulous cook but didn't part with many of her recipes, this being one. As a wedding gift to Gene and me when we were married in 1963, she invited me to her apartment to watch her make this treasured salad dressing. She threw in 'a little of this and a little of that' while I feverishly took notes. She asked me not to share the recipe with anyone. When my husband died, I realized that the recipe would die with me, and I didn't want that to happen and so I shared the recipe with my family – and now with you! The recipe stores well in the refrigerator for months. It is good on many things – salad of course, but is especially delicious served in an avocado – we cut the avocado in half, remove the pit, and fill the hole with the dressing. Through the years, I've adapted the recipe, varying amounts from time to time.

"Tomatoes" by Elaine Abrams

Martha's Spaghetti Sauce

Ingredients
1 - 2 country pork ribs
1/4 cup olive oil
5 - 6 cloves of garlic, thinly sliced (or more if you like it garlicky)
4 large cans crushed tomatoes (1 can be whole peeled tomatoes hand crushed,
    or tomato sauce)
3 small cans tomato paste
1 large can of water (or more if too thick)
Fennel seeds, about 30 or so, crushed
Parsley, about a 1/4 cup, chopped fresh
Basil, about a tablespoon, chopped fresh
1 tablespoon of sugar
Salt and pepper, to taste
1 cup of grated Locatelli cheese (you can add more of this if you like, I like a lot of cheese)

Directions
1. Sear the pork rib on all sides in the olive oil.
2. Add sliced garlic, sauté for about 1 minute (do not burn the garlic).
3. Add the crushed tomatoes, tomato paste, water, herbs, spices and cheese.
4. Simmer for anywhere from 2-1/2 - 3 hours.

Tip
• You can also add raw sausage and cook that in the sauce and/or meatballs, too.

Recipe provided by Martha Mazeika

"Rooster" by Paul McMahon

Mediterranean Chicken Salad

Ingredients

4 chicken breasts, boneless, skinless
1 tablespoon chopped shallots
1/2 cup olive oil
2 teaspoons fresh thyme, finely chopped (or 1 teaspoon dried)
3 teaspoons fresh parsley, chopped fine
Juice of 1/2 medium lemon (1/4 cup)
3/4 cup pitted small black olives (preferably Kalamata)
2 tablespoons capers
10 cherry tomatoes, quartered
1/4 lb. fresh-cooked, pencil-thin asparagus, cut in lengths of 1 inch
    (al dente and still bright green)
1/2 teaspoon fresh ground pepper

Directions

1. Season chicken breasts lightly with salt and pepper and bake in a 375 degree oven for 15 minutes.
2. Tear chicken into strips or cut into pieces. Cool.
3. Toss with olive oil, herbs, lemon juice, capers and shallots.
4. Mix with asparagus, tomatoes and olives. Serves 4.

Recipe provided by Charlene Tyler

"Egg Shell I, II, III" by Claudia Kaufman

Meri's Caesar Salad & Dressing

Ingredients

For Croutons:
Fresh French bread (can use sourdough,
    focaccia, even fresh bagels; must be
    chewy and soft inside)
Garlic powder
Onion powder
Salt and pepper, to taste
1/2 cup extra-virgin olive oil (can be herb
    flavored, such as basil or rosemary)

For Salad:
2 - 3 heads romaine lettuce
Parmesan reggiano
Lemon-infused olive oil

For Dressing:
4 garlic cloves
2 tins anchovy filets rolled with capers
3 fresh whole eggs, coddled
1-1/2 lemons
3 tablespoons dijon or stone ground mustard
5 tablespoons Worcestershire sauce
1/2 cup balsamic vinegar
1-1/2 cups extra-virgin olive oil
6 drops Tabasco sauce

Directions

1. *For Croutons:* Cut bread into large cubes (about 1-1/2 - 2" cubes).
2. Put in large bowl. Cover evenly with olive oil. Sprinkle liberally with garlic and onion powder. Add salt and pepper to taste. Gently mix to cover bread cubes.
3. Coat the bottom of a large cast iron frying pan with olive oil (no more than 1/8" deep). Set on medium high heat; once hot, sear the croutons in batches, turn to brown all sides, do not blacken.
4. While frying, continue to add garlic and onion powder and/or salt to taste, for preferred intensity of flavor.
5. *For Dressing:* Add all dressing ingredients, except coddled eggs, into a blender and blend on high for several minutes. Sample and adjust vinegar/oil balance to taste.
6. Slowly add one coddled egg at a time, blending until dressing achieves desired thickness (may not need third egg).
7. *For Salad:* Wash and dry lettuce leaves. Tear into bite size pieces and place in large serving bowl.
8. Pour on desired amount of dressing (you will have extra) and toss to coat lettuce.
9. Top liberally with shaved or coarsely grated parmesan.
10. Place croutons on top. Finish with a light lemon oil drizzle.

Recipe provided by Marianne Murphy

"Bowl of Limons" by Claudia Kaufman

Potato Salad

Ingredients

1-1/2 lbs. of boiling potatoes, quartered lengthwise and cut crosswise into 3/4" slices
1 tablespoon kosher salt
1/4 cup fresh lemon juice, divided as noted below
1 red bell pepper, roasted and diced or 1/2 cup drained and diced bottled pimento
1/2 cup pitted black or kalamata olives
3 scallions, minced
3/4 teaspoon dried oregano
1/2 cup olive oil
1 cup of feta cheese or more

Directions

1. Steam or boil potatoes until tender and transfer to a large bowl.
2. Toss the potatoes with kosher salt and 2 tablespoons of the lemon juice, cool.
3. Add the red pepper, olives and scallions.
4. In a small bowl, whisk together the remaining 2 tablespoons lemon juice and the oregano, add the olive oil in a stream, whisking until it is emulsified.
5. Pour the dressing over the potatos, toss. Season with additional salt and pepper as needed.
6. Add feta cheese just before serving. Serves 4.

Tip

• The salad keeps, covered and chilled, overnight.

Recipe provided by Charlene Tyler

"Ratatouille Quartet" by Frank Costantino

Salata Kuthra

Dressing Ingredients

Make before preparing vegetables, and let settle

1 part olive oil

2 parts fresh-squeezed lemon juice

Sprinkle in generous pinches of dried thyme

Salad Ingredients

3 tomatoes, chopped, or ¾ cup cherry tomatoes, sliced

1 green pepper, chopped

1/2 avocado, cubed

1/2 cucumber, peeled & chopped

Directions

1. Mix olive oil, lemon juice and thyme, stir. Make dressing first and let settle.
2. Chop vegetables and combine in bowl.
3. Add dressing to vegetables just before serving.

Tip

• Salad quantity can be extended by adding a pita bread, cubed.

Recipe provided by Diana Hosley Burchfield

"My weaknesses have always been food and men — in that order."   ~Dolly Parton

"Cabbage & Swiss Chard" by Frank Costantino

Spinach Salad with Warm Bacon Dressing

Dressing Ingredients

5 or 6 slices of bacon
2 eggs
2/3 cup sugar
2/3 cup water
2/3 cup apple cider vinegar
2 - 3 tablespoons flour
Salt and pepper, to taste

Salad Ingredients

Spinach leaves, torn into bite size pieces
White button mushrooms, thinly sliced
Red onion, thinly sliced
Hard boiled eggs, sliced
Croutons

Dressing Directions

1. Cook the bacon in a skillet until moderately crisp. Remove cooked bacon and place on paper towels. Do not discard the bacon grease. Set pan aside to cool slightly. (You will be adding the egg mixture to this grease and if it is too hot the eggs will cook too much.)
2. In a separate bowl, beat the eggs, sugar, water, apple cider vinegar, flour, salt and pepper until well combined and there are no lumps from the flour.
3. Place the pan with the bacon grease back on the stove on a low flame. Slowly add the egg mixture while whisking thoroughly to combine. Stir constantly until the mixture thickens to your desired consistency.
4. Chop the cooked bacon into small pieces and add it to the finished warm dressing; reserve some for garnish on top of the salad.

Salad Directions

1. Place washed spinach leaves in a bowl. Add sliced hard boiled eggs, white button mushrooms and very thinly sliced red onion. Sprinkle salad with croutons if desired.
2. Pour Bacon Dressing over salad while warm. The greens will wilt slightly.
3. Garnish with chopped bacon pieces. Serve immediately.

Recipe provided by Mimi Ahmed Knittle
Growing up in Pennsylvania, on the edge of Amish country, this Warm Bacon Dressing recipe is a tradition. You can use the dressing on a salad or poured over boiled cut up potatoes for a Warm Pennsylvania Dutch Potato Salad.

"Rhubarb & Berries" by Frank Costantino

Strawberry Rhubarb Chutney

Ingredients

1 tablespoon extra-virgin olive oil
1 cup diced red onion
6 tablespoons blackberry vinegar (can also use raspberry or mixed berry vinegar)
1 tablespoon finely chopped peeled fresh ginger
3 cloves roasted garlic
1 cup dried blueberries (can also use dried cranberries or golden raisins)
Pinch of chipotle spice
1/4 teaspoon sea salt
8 tablespoons brown sugar
Finely grated zest of 1 large orange
1/2 cup fresh orange juice
1/2 cup water
2 cups rhubarb cut into 1/2" pieces
4 cups strawberries, cut into 1/2" pieces

Directions

1. Put the olive oil into a large non-reactive pot (such as a Le Creuset) and set the pot over medium heat. When hot, stir in the red onion and pour on the berry vinegar. Stir well and cook about 5 minutes, until onion is almost tender. The vinegar keeps the onion bright.
2. Add the ginger, garlic, blueberries, chipotle and salt, and cook about 1 minute, stirring.
3. Add the brown sugar, orange zest, orange juice and water, mix together and cook another minute.
4. Drop in the rhubarb, stir well and cover the pan. Cook 4 - 5 minutes, stirring once or twice, just until the rhubarb starts to break up. Add the strawberries, stir, and cover the pan again. Cook 2 - 3 minutes, until the berries soften.
5. Uncover the pot and simmer on medium low heat for up to 10 minutes. Chutney is done when the mixture thickens and a spoon leaves a trail along the bottom of the pot.

Tip

• Delicious served over chicken or duck.

Recipe provided by Robin Taliesin

"Let's Eat" by Louis Rizzo

Superfine BBQ Sauce

Ingredients

1 medium onion, peeled and quartered
1/4 cup water
1 cup ketchup
5 tablespoons molasses
2 tablespoons cider vinegar
2 tablespoons Worcestershire sauce
2 tablespoons dijon mustard
1 teaspoon hot sauce
1/4 teaspoon ground pepper
2 tablespoons canola oil
1 medium clove of garlic, minced
1 teaspoon chili powder
1/4 teaspoon cayenne pepper

Directions

1. Process the onion with the water in a food processor until pureed and resembles slush.
2. Strain mixture through fine mesh strainer, pressing to extract all liquid to obtain 1/2 cup of juice. Discard solids.
3. Whisk onion juice, ketchup, molasses, vinegar, Worcestershire, mustard, hot sauce and black pepper in a medium bowl.
4. Heat oil in a non-reactive pot over medium heat. Add garlic, chili powder and cayenne.
5. Cook until fragrant – about 30 seconds. Whisk in the ketchup mixture and bring to a boil.
6. Reduce heat and simmer until reduced – about 25 minutes. Cool before using.

Tips

• Store in the refrigerator in an airtight container for up to a week.
• Yields 1-1/2 cups.

Recipe provided by Superfine Restaurant
www.superfinefood.com | 126 Washington Street, Marblehead

"Shubie's" by Stephanie Krauss Verdun

Tabouli

Ingredients
2-1/2 lbs. bulgar wheat
2 bay leaves
2 english cucumbers, halved, cut each half into thirds lengthwise
2 pints grape tomatoes, quartered
1 bunch flat leaf parsley, chopped
1 red onion, small diced
1/2 - 1 bunch fresh mint, chopped
1/2 bunch dill, chopped
1/2 cup fresh lemon juice, plus a splash for the bulgar
1 cup extra virgin olive oil
1/4 cup white wine vinegar
2 tablespoons lemon zest
1-1/2 teaspoons aleppo chili pepper
Oregano to taste
Salt to taste

Directions
1. Cook the bulgur wheat in water with 2 bay leaves, a little lemon juice and salt. When finished cooking, drain and let cool.
2. Once the bulgur is cool, combine with all the remaining ingredients and adjust seasoning to taste.

Tip
• Serve with pita bread or pita chips and enjoy!

Recipe provided by Doug Shube of Shubie's
www.shubies.com | 16 Atlantic Avenue, Marblehead

"I have made a lot of mistakes falling in love, and regretted most of them, but never the potatoes that went with them."   ~Nora Ephron

Soups & Sides

"Boiled Peanuts" by Patricia Dunbar

Aunt Arlene's Peanut Soup

Ingredients

1/2 stick unsalted butter
1 medium onion
2 celery ribs
3 tablespoons flour
8 cups chicken stock
2 cups smooth peanut butter
1-3/4 cups light cream (can also use half & half)
Salted peanuts, chopped

Directions

1. Melt the butter in a soup pot over medium heat. Add finely chopped onion and celery, stir often, cook until soft, 3 - 5 minutes. Stir in flour, cook 2 minutes longer.
2. Pour in chicken stock, increase heat to high, bring to a boil, stirring constantly. Reduce heat to medium and cook, stirring often, until slightly reduced and thickened, about 15 minutes. Strain hard through sieve.
3. Return liquid to pot, whisk peanut butter and cream into liquid. Warm over low heat, whisking often, about 5 minutes. Do not boil.
4. Serve warm. Garnish with chopped, salted peanuts.

Recipe provided by Robin Taliesin
Whenever my Aunt made this for our holiday gatherings, I would
want so many helpings I wasn't hungry for the rest of the meal!

"If you're afraid of butter, use cream."

~Julia Child

"Squash" by Barbara Naeser

Butternut Squash, Red Grapes & Sage

Ingredients
2-1/4 lbs. butternut squash, in 1-1/2" pieces
1-1/2 cups red grapes (8 oz.)
1 medium onion in 1" pieces
1 tablespoon fresh sage leaves, sliced
2 tablespoons olive oil
2 tablespoons melted butter
1/4 cup toasted pine nuts

Directions
1. Preheat oven to 425 degrees.
2. Mix everything except pine nuts in large bowl. Toss to coat.
3. Spread in large rimmed baking dish. Roast until squash and onion begin to brown, stirring occasionally, about 50 minutes.
4. Transfer to platter, sprinkle with pine nuts and serve. Makes 4 - 6 servings.

Recipe provided by Ann Welch

"If more of us valued food and cheer and song above hoarded gold, it would be a merrier world."

~J.R.R. Tolkien

"Spam" by Polly Maxon Tritschler

California Spam Fried Rice

Ingredients

1 tablespoon butter
1/2 (12 oz.) can Spam Classic, cut in cubes
3 large eggs
2 cups cooked green beans, cut into 1/8" pieces
2 tablespoons canola oil
4 tablespoons soy sauce
1 small onion, chopped
2 cloves garlic, minced
4 cups chilled cooked rice

Directions

1. In a small frying pan, melt butter. Add eggs, cook, chopping into small pieces with spatula until scrambled.
2. In a deep frying pan, heat oil over high heat. Add onion and cook 3 - 4 minutes or until translucent.
3. Add garlic and stir-fry 30 seconds longer.
4. Add Spam Classic, cook 3 minutes more.
5. Add beans, rice, egg and soy sauce and stir until heated through. Serve immediately. Serves 4 - 6.

Recipe provided by Polly Maxon Tritschler

"Whenever you see the word cuisine used instead of the word food, be prepared to pay an additional eighty percent." ~George Carlin

"On Its Own Terms" by Janet Albert

Coconut Leek Soup

Ingredients

3-1/2 cups chopped white and pale green leeks, washed first
1 medium cauliflower, florets, separated from stalks and core, chopped
1 cup chopped onion
2 tablespoons coconut oil or butter
1 tablespoon chopped garlic
1 teaspoon peeled, grated ginger root
1/4 teaspoon grated or ground nutmeg
2 cups chicken or vegetable broth
2 cups canned coconut milk
Dash of fish sauce (optional)

Directions

1. Saute leeks, cauliflower, and onion in coconut oil or butter on medium-low heat until softened, about 5 minutes, stirring occasionally.
2. Add garlic and ginger, cook, stirring for a few minutes; don't let it get dark.
3. Add coconut milk and broth; bring to a boil, then simmer for 20 minutes, stirring occasionally.
4. Add salt and pepper to taste, fish sauce, and nutmeg.
5. Cool slightly, then blend in 2 batches in blender.
6. Taste for seasoning, add more salt and pepper if necessary. Makes 4-6 servings.

Recipe provided by Janet Albert

"Marsh" by Mimi Ahmed Knittle

Cream of Curried Pea Soup

Ingredients
1 cup shelled fresh peas
1 medium onion, sliced
1 small carrot, sliced
1 stalk celery with leaves, sliced
1 medium potato, sliced
1 clove garlic
1 teaspoon salt
1 teaspoon curry powder
2 cups chicken stock
1 cup cream

Directions
1. Place the vegetables, seasonings and one cup stock in saucepan and bring to a boil. Cover, reduce the heat and simmer for 15 minutes.
2. Transter to the container of an electric blender. Cover and turn on high speed. Remove the cover and with the motor running, pour in the remaining stock and cream.
3. Chill and serve topped with whipped cream.

Recipe provided by Patricia Dunbar

"Abstract" by Carin Doben

Easy Gazpacho

Ingredients
1 clove of garlic
1 small onion
1 green pepper
1-1/2 cups tomato juice, chilled
1 cucumber peeled and sliced
2 medium tomatoes seeded and quartered
   -or- 1 large can peeled tomatoes
1 teaspoon salt
1/4 teaspoon pepper
1 cup chilled chicken bouillon
2 tablespoons olive oil
3 tablespoons red wine vinegar

Directions
1. Blend first 3 Ingredients and 1/2 cup tomato juice in Cuisinart until chopped.
2. Add cucumber, tomatoes, salt and pepper. Pulse until chopped but not too smooth.
3. Add remaining tomato juice, bouillon, oil and vinegar. Chill well.

Recipe provided by Carin Doben

"Eggplant" by Amy Hourihan

Grilled Eggplant & Cherry Tomatoes

Ingredients
2 tablespoons olive oil
1-1/2 lbs. italian eggplant, sliced, skins can remain on
1 pint cherry tomatoes, cut in half
4 cloves garlic, coarsely chopped
1 yellow onion, sliced thinly
1 sprig fresh thyme
1 sprig fresh oregano
1 sprig fresh basil
Salt and pepper
Vegetable grilling pan, perforated

Directions
1. Set grill to moderate/high heat. Place a vegetable grill basket on grill and heat.
2. Using tongs and a folded paper towel, dipped in olive oil, grease the grill basket to prevent vegetables from sticking.
3. Add the eggplant, tomatoes, garlic and onion to the grill pan in a thin layer, working in batches, turning frequently about 5 minutes per side. (Do not overload the pan, as vegetables will steam rather than grill).
4. Add the sprigs of herbs to the cooking vegetables, and when toasted, strip the leaves from the stems, and mince them, set aside.
5. Remove vegetables from the grill to a bowl, and toss with salt, pepper and one tablespoon of olive oil. Add toasted herbs and continue tossing.

Tips
• Add to warm pasta or use as a topping for pizza.
• Can also be served at room temperature as a side dish.
• Excellent with feta cheese and as an accompaniment with fish or grilled meats.

Recipe provided by Amy Hourihan

"Herring Creek" by Mimi Ahmed Knittle

Hobo Beans

Ingredients

2 or 3 onions, chopped
1/2 lb. ground beef
1/2 lb. bacon
1 can butter beans
1 can kidney beans
2 cans baked beans
1 tablespoon vinegar
1/2 cup sugar
1/2 cup brown sugar
1 cup ketchup

Directions

1. Brown onion and ground beef. Set aside.
2. Cook bacon until crisp, drain fat.
3. Combine with onion and ground beef in a crock pot or large bowl.
4. Drain liquid from beans and add to beef/onion mixture.
5. Add rest of ingredients and mix.

Tip

• I cook on low in crock pot for whenever… or you can bake in oven at 350 degrees for an hour. Enjoy, take BEANO!!

Recipe provided by Chrissie Greatrex

"Tomato Gang" by Claudia Kaufman

Italian Sausage Soup

Ingredients
1-1/2 cups coarsely chopped celery
1-1/2 cups chopped onions
1 clove garlic
3 tablespoons olive oil
2 cups canned Italian tomatoes, chopped and with liquid
1 cup tomato puree
1-1/4 lbs. Italian sausage, sauteed & drained
6 cups chicken broth
1/2 teaspoon oregano
2 bay leaves
1/2 teaspoon thyme
1/2 cup chopped parsley
3 tablespoons sugar
1 cup orzo or other small pasta
Grated fresh parmesan for garnish

Directions
1. Saute celery, onions and garlic in olive oil.
2. Add tomatoes, puree and sausage. Cook 10 minutes over medium heat.
3. Add broth, herbs and sugar. Simmer 30 minutes longer.
4. Add pasta and continue cooking until just done. Serves 8 - 10.

Tips
• Sometimes I need to thin this down with more chicken broth.
• Do not increase amount of pasta if using orzo.

Recipe provided by Ann Welch

"Red Beets" by Kirsten Fischler

Kirsten's Ukrainian American Winter Borscht

Ingredients

1/2 package smoked Turkey Kobasa (Kielbasa) chopped or uncooked sausage out of its casing.

3 medium beets, peeled and shredded (I like to mix two red and one golden)

2 carrots, peeled and shredded

6 large radish quartered (radish becomes sweet when cooked)

3 medium baking potatoes, peeled, 1/2" cubes

1 tablespoon olive oil

1 medium white onion, chopped or red for a stronger flavor

1 (6 oz.) can tomato paste

1-1/2 quarts chicken stock (or beef stock)

1/2 cup red wine (A Spanish Rioja is a good choice, then pour a glass to enjoy)

1/2 medium head purple cabbage, cored and shredded

2 medium or 1-1/2 large tomatoes diced and drained (Brandywine or Beefsteak)

3 or 4 medium cloves garlic, minced and pressed

Sea salt and pepper to taste

1 teaspoon smoked paprika, sweet (pimento´n dulce) or spicy for oomph!

1/4 teaspoon coriander

1/4 teaspoon cumin

Real New England maple syrup to taste

1/2 cup sour cream, for topping (regular or low fat)

2 tablespoons fresh parsley chopped

Directions

1. Place the chopped Kielbasa or crumble the sausage into a skillet over medium-high heat. Cook the Kielbasa until lightly brown or cook the raw sausage and stir until no longer pink. The Turkey Kielbasa will need a little oil in the pan whereas the raw pork sausage has its own fat. Remove from the heat and set aside.

2. Fill a large pot halfway with 1-1/2 - 2 quarts of chicken stock and bring to a boil. The amount of chicken stock depends on how thick you like your borscht, less or more broth will make a stew versus a soup. Add the sausage and cover the pot. Return to a boil. Add the smoked paprika, cumin and coriander.

3. Add the beets and cook until they have lost their color. Add the radish, carrots and potatoes, and cook until tender, about 15 minutes. Add the cabbage, and the diced tomato.

4. Heat the oil in a skillet over medium heat. Add the onion and cook until tender.

5. Stir the tomato paste and red wine until well blended. Transfer to the pot.

6. Add the raw garlic to the soup, cover and turn off the heat. Let stand for 5 minutes.

7. Taste and season, with sea salt, pepper and real maple syrup, ladle into serving bowls, and garnish with sour cream and fresh parsley.

Recipe provided by Kirsten Fischler
This is my contemporary American take on my Ukrainian grandmother's borscht.
The "summer borscht" does not have meat or potatoes and is served cold.

"Paris Vegetable Study" by Charlie Allen

Potato & Leek Soup

Ingredients
3 tablespoons unsalted butter
1 small Vidalia onion, chopped fine
3 medium leeks, rinsed and chopped
1 medium carrot, chopped (optional)
1 cup Cremini mushrooms, chopped (optional)
2 medium Yukon Gold potatoes, cut in 1" pieces
1 teaspoon salt
1/4 teaspoon pepper
1 garlic clove, minced
16 oz. chicken or vegetable stock
3 slices bacon, rendered and crisped, chopped fine
2/3 cup light cream

Directions
1. Melt butter in large saucepan over medium heat. Add onion, leeks, carrot, mushrooms, potatoes, salt, pepper and garlic. Cook until tender, about 10 minutes.
2. Transfer vegetables to Dutch oven, add stock and bacon. Bring to boil. Reduce heat and simmer until softened, 15 - 20 minutes.
3. Transfer soup to blender using ladle. Blend until completely smooth. Return soup to now empty pot.
4. Stir in cream and bring to simmer. Add more cream if needed. Season with salt and pepper to taste.

Tip
• Garnish with chopped chives and sour cream.

Recipe provided by Charlie Allen

"Three Golden Beets" by Kirsten Fischler

Red & Gold Beets with Whipped Cheese Filling

Ingredients

12 oz. whipped cream cheese or crème fraîche
12 oz. plain goat cheese
Pint of whipping cream (can also use heavy cream)
2 tablespoons fresh chives, minced, plus some whole strands for garnish
1 tablespoon fresh basil, minced, plus some whole leaves for garnish
Grated lemon zest, 1/2 of a lemon rind
1/2 teaspoon salt
3 red beets, fresh
3 gold beets, fresh
Orange- or lemon-infused olive oil

Directions

1. *For Filling:* Whip the cream until it forms very stiff peaks. Place aside.
2. Place whipped cream cheese and goat cheese in a large bowl and stir until completely blended. Fold whipped cream into cheese mixture. Do not over-stir, result should be fluffy.
3. Add minced chives and basil, half of the grated lemon zest and salt; mix gently.
4. *For Beets:* Wrap beets in foil, keeping colors separate, and place on baking tray. Bake in 400 degree oven for an hour, until a fork can pierce beet with a little resistance.
5. Remove from oven and let cool just until they can be handled. While still warm, peel skins off beets (keeping colors separate) under running water or in a bowl of water.
6. Slice beets into 1/2" thick rounds. Let cool to room temperature.
7. On a serving platter, arrange all red beet rounds.
8. Carefully spoon about 3 tablespoons of the cheese filling onto each red beet round.
9. Lay a similarly sized round of gold beet over the filling and press gently to set. The amount of filling between the beet slices should be equivalent in height (about 1/2") to the beets.
10. Drizzle the citrus-infused oil over the beet platter and sprinkle the remaining grated lemon zest over all. Garnish with a few chive strands and some basil leaves. Serve at room temperature.

Tip

• Both beets and filling can be prepared a day in advance but don't plate them together until you are ready to serve.

Recipe provided by Marianne Murphy

"Staying In Touch" by Janet Albert

Spicy Tomato & Fish Stew

Ingredients

1/2 teaspoon saffron threads
1 tablespoon boiling water
2 cups crushed canned Italian plum tomatoes
3 tablespoons olive oil
1/2 teaspoon smoked paprika
1/2 teaspoon crushed red pepper flakes
2 cups chicken stock
Salt, to taste
1 lb. haddock, hake or halibut, cut into 2" pieces
8 large shrimp, peeled, deveined
Handful fresh oregano springs, leaves chopped
Dash or two of fish sauce

Directions

1. In small bowl, combine saffron and 1/2 the water; using back of small spoon, crush saffron; add remaining water, set aside for 1 hour.
2. In large flameproof casserole, heat 2 tablespoons of oil over medium heat. Add paprika and red pepper; cook, stirring, for 1 minute. Add tomatoes, stir well, cover pan; Cook 1 minute.
3. Remove lid, stir again, and add saffron, stock, and salt, add fish sauce to taste. Bring to a boil, cover and simmer 10 minutes.
4. Add the fish and shrimp; make sure fish are submerged. Sprinkle with 1/2 of the oregano. Return to a boil; lower heat, and cover pan.
5. Simmer 8 minutes, cooking and stirring *gently* so fish doesn't break up.
6. Taste for seasoning; add more salt or fish sauce, if you like. Sprinkle with remaining oregano. Serves 4.

Recipe provided by Janet Albert

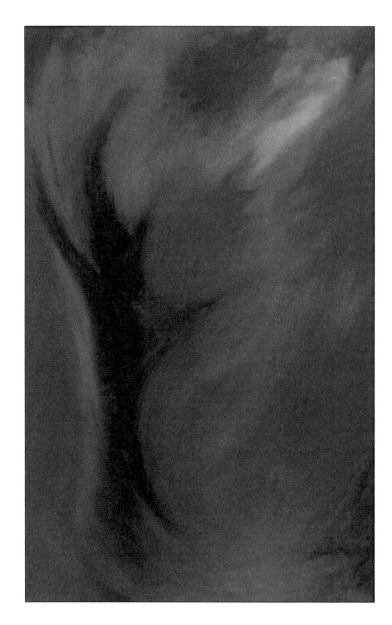

"Blackheart" by Robin Taliesin

Sweet Potato Souffle

Ingredients
6 medium sweet potatoes
3 tablespoons butter
2 eggs, beaten
1/2 teaspoon salt
1/4 cup light brown sugar
1/4 cup sugar
1/4 cup dried coconut flakes
Cinnamon, to taste

Directions
1. Preheat oven to 350 degrees.
2. Bake the sweet potatoes until cooked, peel then mash.
2. Add butter and eggs to mashed potatoes, beat until light and fluffy.
3. Add all remaining ingredients, reserving some of the coconut.
4. Place in a buttered 2 quart casserole dish and sprinkle with cinnamon.
5. Bake for about 30 minutes.
6. Just before removing from oven, sprinkle with remaining coconut and brown.

Recipe provided by Claudia Kaufman

"Cooking is like love. It should be entered into with abandon or not at all."

~Harriet van Horne

"Farmer's Market" by Patricia Dunbar

Veggie Pie

Ingredients
4 eggs, beaten
3 cups veggies (your choice: zucchini, green beans, corn, mushrooms, etc.)
1 medium chopped onion
1/2 cup vegetable oil
1/2 cup grated Parmesan cheese (more for topping)
1 cup Bisquick (or 1 cup flour + 1/2 teaspoon baking soda + 1/4 teaspoon salt)
Salt, pepper and parsley to taste

Directions
1. Preheat oven to 350 degrees.
2. Combine all ingredients, place in oven-proof 10" pie plate or casserole dish.
3. Cover the top with additional grated Parmesan cheese.
4. Bake for 40 minutes or until cake tester comes out clean.

Tip
• Optional: garnish top with mushroom slices.

Recipe provided by Sandra Golbert

"Vegetables are a must on a diet. I suggest carrot cake, zucchini bread and pumpkin pie."

~Jim Davis

"The only time to eat diet food is while you're waiting for the steak to cook." ~Julia Child

Entrees

"Blue Lobster" by Mimi Ahmed Knittle

Aunt Ginny's Seafood Casserole

Ingredients
1/2 lb. mushrooms, sliced
8 tablespoons butter
1 lb. cooked shrimp, or a little more if desired
2 cups lobster meat, or a little more if desired
1/4 cup sherry, dry
4 tablespoons flour
2 cups light cream
Salt and pepper
3/4 cup bread crumbs (or use crumbled cornflakes)

Directions
1. Saute the mushrooms in 2 tablespoons butter for 10 minutes until soft but not brown.
2. Place shrimp and lobster in the top of a double boiler with 1 tablespoon butter and sherry. Heat over boiling water for 10 - 15 minutes.
3. Meanwhile, make sauce by melting 4 tablespoons of butter, blending in 4 tablespoons flour and cream. Bring to a boil, stirring constantly. Season with salt and pepper. Simmer for 5 minutes.
4. Combine mushrooms, seafood and sauce and put in a casserole or dish that can be used for serving. Cover with breadcrumbs (or cornflakes); dot with butter. Bake at 375 degrees for 20 - 30 minutes, or until the top is brown.

Tip
• This can be served over rice, or on toast points or pastry shells.

Recipe provided by Julie Livingston

"Fresh Fish" by Louis Rizzo

Baked Cod

Ingredients
1-1/2 lbs. fresh codfish
5+ slices firm bread (oatmeal bread is good)
Enough white flour to cover fish
Enough skim milk to cover fish (reconstituted milk is okay)
Herbs de Provence

Directions
1. Toast bread, then cut into cubes 1/2 inch square.
2. Rinse fish with water, pat dry, dredge with white flour (check for little bones and remove them).
3. Place fish lengthwise in glass loaf dish.
4. Pour in milk to cover fish.
5. Add toasted bread cubes on top of fish.
6. Sprinkle Herbs de Provence on top of bread cubes on fish.
7. Bake at 350 degrees for about one hour. Fish is done if skewer inserts easily.
   Serves about 4.

Tips
• Preheat oven to 350 degrees.
• Glass loaf dish required (approximately 6 x 9 x 3").

Recipe provided by Diana Hosley Burchfield

"School of Fish" by Amy Hourihan

Baked Salmon with Mustard-Crumb Crust

Ingredients

2 tablespoons plus 1 teaspoon white wine vinegar
1 tablespoon sugar
2 heaping tablespoons dijon mustard
1-1/2 teaspoons dry mustard
1/3 cup canola oil or other vegetable oil
4 - 6 pieces salmon filets, about 6 ounces each
Dried thyme
Salt and freshly ground pepper
1 cup fresh bread crumbs, crushed Pepperidge Farm stuffing mix, or panko

Directions

1. Place vinegar, sugar and both mustards in small food processor or blender. With machine running, slowly pour in oil and blend until medium-thick sauce forms (can be made several days in advance and refrigerated).
2. Preheat oven to 375 degrees. Lightly grease baking dish or baking pan lined with aluminum foil. Arrange salmon in dish, skin side down. Sprinkle each piece with dried thyme, salt and pepper. Spread 1 tablespoon mustard sauce over each filet, covering completely. Press crumbs or panko onto fish.
3. Bake salmon until cooked through and top is crisp and golden, about 16 - 18 minutes depending on the thickness of the salmon.
4. Serve hot, cold, or at room temperature.

Recipe provided by Judy Jacobi
This is an adaptation of a Bon Appetit recipe from the 90's!

"Hanging Red Peppers" by Barbara Naeser

Cajun Shrimp

Ingredients

1 lb. shrimp (your choice as to the size) – peeled and deveined
5 tablespoons butter
4 teaspoons Worcestershire sauce
1-1/2 teaspoons chili powder
1/4 teaspoon cayenne pepper
2 cloves garlic, minced
1/4 cup red wine
1/2 teaspoon salt
2 teaspoons black pepper

Directions

1. Preheat oven to 425 degrees.
2. Arrange shrimp in one layer in an oven proof baking dish.
3. Combine all other ingredients in a small saucepan.
4. Heat ingredients on a medium heat and simmer for several minutes – until the butter has melted. Pour mixture over shrimp.
5. Bake shrimp with spice mixture for 6 - 8 minutes or until the shrimp has turned pink.
6. Serve over rice. Enjoy!

Recipe provided by Christine Nuccio
This is a simple but spicy dish that is quick to prepare and always receives rave reviews.

"Brahma" by Paul McMahon

Chicken Pot Pie

Ingredients

4 whole boneless, skinless chicken breasts (2 lbs.)
1 cup heavy cream
4 carrots, peeled and cut into 1/2" pieces
2 zucchini, unpeeled cut into 1/2" pieces
5 tablespoons unsalted butter
2 small yellow onions, coarsely chopped
5 tablespoons flour
1 cup canned chicken broth

1/4 cup cognac or dry white wine
1 tablespoon dried tarragon
1-1/2 teaspoons salt
1/2 teaspoon ground black pepper
1 egg
1 tablespoon water
1 refrigerated pie crust

Directions

1. Preheat oven 350 degrees. Place the chicken breasts in a single layer in a baking pan. Pour the cream over the chicken and bake 20 - 25 minutes.
2. Remove the chicken from the cream, reserve the cream and cooking juices. Let the chicken cool and cut into 1 inch pieces.
3. Blanch the carrots in boiling salted water for 3 minutes. Add the zucchini and cook 1 minute more. Rinse under cool water, drain.
4. Melt the butter in a large saucepan over medium heat. Add the onions and sauté until translucent, about 5 minutes. Add the flour and cook stirring constantly for 5 minutes. Do not let the flour brown.
5. Add the chicken broth and cook stirring constantly until thickened. Stir in the reserved cream and cooking juices and the cognac. Cook over low heat until thick, about 5 minutes.
6. Stir in the tarragon, salt and pepper and simmer 1 minute. Add the chicken and vegetables and mix gently into the cream sauce. Remove from the heat.
7. Pre-mix the egg and water in a small bowl. Place the chicken and vegetable mixture into a deep, 2 quart casserole dish. Put the pastry on top and trim, brush the edge of the dish with the egg wash and press overhanging dough onto the dish. Brush the top of the pastry with the egg wash and cut a steam hole in the center to vent.
8. Place casserole on a baking sheet and bake on the middle rack until the crust is golden, 20 - 25 minutes. Serve immediately. Makes 6 portions.

Recipe provided by Chrissie Greatrex
An adaptation of an old Silver Palate recipe.

"Rooster" by Beverly Seamans

Country Captain Chicken

Ingredients
1 broiler, fryer chicken, cut
1 teaspoon salt
1/4 teaspoon pepper
1/4 cup butter
1 medium onion, chopped
1 clove garlic, crushed
2 teaspoons curry powder
1/2 teaspoon thyme
1 can (1 lb.) tomatoes
1/4 cup raisins
Hot cooked rice
Toasted blanched almonds
Chutney

Directions
1. Sprinkle chicken pieces on both sides with salt and pepper.
2. Heat butter in large skillet, add onion, garlic, curry and thyme.
3. Cook until onion is tender but not brown.
4. Add tomatoes, raisins and chicken.
5. Cook, covered, 20 - 30 minutes until chicken is tender.
6. Serve over rice with almonds and chutney. Serves 4.

Tip
• Cooking time: 30 minutes.

Recipe provided by Patricia Dunbar

"Crab" by Mimi Ahmed Knittle

Country Club Crab Cakes

Ingredients
1 lb. of cleaned crabmeat (drained well)
1/4 cup mayonnaise
1 teaspoon prepared mustard (not dijon)
1 teaspoon Old Bay seasoning
1/2 teaspoon Worcestershire sauce
1/2 teaspoon black pepper
1 egg, beaten
1/4 cup bread crumbs (more or less, as needed)
Butter

Directions
1. Gently fold all ingredients until combined being careful not to break up the crab too much. Add the 1/4 cup bread crumbs until the mixture comes together.
2. *For Crab Cakes:* form the mixture into the size cakes you desire; spray a cookie sheet with oil and place individual crab cakes onto sheet; drizzle a bit of melted butter onto the top of each cake; bake at 350 degrees for approximately 20 minutes until slightly golden brown (makes 5 large four oz. each Crab Cakes).
3. *For Crab Puffs:* form into 1 oz. balls; place on a cookie sheet sprayed with oil; drizzle with a bit of melted butter; bake at 350 degrees for approximately 10 minutes until slightly golden brown (makes about 20 Crab Puffs).
4. Serve with lemon wedges, cocktail sauce or tarter sauce.

Tips
• You can use fresh crab from the seafood market or canned crab but try to combine lump crab with the smaller pieces of crab for the best consistency and flavor.
• Recipe can be doubled or tripled!

Recipe provided by Mimi Ahmed Knittle
These crab cakes are always served as an appetizer at our family holiday gatherings.

"The Watering Hole" by Paul McMahon

Curry Chicken Delight

Ingredients

2 - 3 lb. cut up chicken filets or 4 whole boneless chicken breasts
   (hammered thin and cut into filets)
1/3 cup flour
8 slices bacon
1 cup honey
8 tablespoons prepared mustard (dijon is best)
1 teaspoon salt
1+ tablespoon(s) curry powder
Hot cooked rice

Directions

1. Preheat oven to 350 degrees.
2. Coat chicken with flour.
3. Cook bacon, drain and crumble.
4. Add chicken to drippings in pan, slowly brown on all sides, 10 minutes.
5. Put chicken in 10" square baking pan. Bake uncovered for 15 - 30 minutes.
6. Combine honey, etc. Pour on chicken. Bake 15 minutes more.
7. Top with crumbled bacon. Serve with rice.

Tip

• I find 30 minutes total for this amount is enough, longer if you double the recipe.

Recipe provided by Brenda Arnold

"Pigasus" by Elaine Caliri Daly

Farfalle & Sausage

Ingredients

12 - 16 oz. sweet or hot sausage, removed from casing
6 tablespoons olive oil
1/2 cup coarsely chopped onion
1 glove of garlic finely chopped
1/4 teaspoon crushed red pepper flakes
6 sundried tomatoes, cut in 1/4" strips
1/2 cup boiling water
(1) 16 oz. box of farfalle pasta
1/2 lb. fresh green beans, cut to 1" pieces
2 tablespoons chopped parsley
Fresh ground pepper

Directions

1. Put sundried tomatoes in hot water for 15 minutes, set aside.
2. Break up sausage and cook until done, set aside.
3. Add oil and onion to hot skillet cook for 5 minutes.
4. Add garlic and brown.
5. Boil the pasta and add green beans the last 4 or 5 minutes of cooking time. Drain.
6. Mix all together, top with parsley and ground pepper.

Tip

• Farfalle are bowties.

Recipe provided by Chrissie Greatrex

"The Ladies" by Paul McMahon

French Pot Roast

Ingredients

2-1/2 lbs. chuck roast
2 tablespoons oil
1/2 cup chopped onions
1/4 cup chopped celery
2 cloves garlic
1/2 cup carrots, cut in 1 inch prices
1/4 cup minced parsley
1 bottle red wine (burgundy)
1 bay leaf
Salt and pepper to taste

Directions

1. Preheat oven to 350 degrees.
2. Trim fat from pot roast. Brown meat in 1 tablespoon oil, in large skillet. Remove from heat.
3. Saute onions, celery and garlic in 1 tablespoon oil.
4. Add meat and vegetables, mix in oven proof casserole with 3" sides.
5. Pour 2 cups wine over the meat. Add bay leaf.
6. Roast for 90 minutes. Check frequently to keep liquid about 1-1/2" deep. Add wine as needed.
7. Continue to cook until tender and meat can be cut with the knife. Serves 6.

Tip

• Serve with roasted potatoes, French bread and a salad.

Recipe provided by Linda Lea Bertrand

"On the Farm" by Paul McMahon

German Pot Roast (Chrissie's Cookie Meat!)

Ingredients

3/4 cup cider vinegar

1/4 cup ketchup

1/2 cup chopped onion

1 teaspoon garlic

(2) 14 oz. cans beef broth

12 ginger snap cookies

(2) 8 oz. envelopes brown gravy mix

Baby carrots and mushrooms

4 - 5 lb. boneless chuck roast

Directions

1. Combine all ingredients except meat, mix well.
2. Add meat, stir to coat.
3. Cover and cook on low for 8 - 10 hours, or on high for 5 hours.
4. Serve over egg noodles. Makes 8 - 10 servings.

Tip

• Use 5 - 7 quart crock pot.

Recipe provided by Chrissie Greatrex

"Garlic" by K. Jean Fisher

Kufta Kebabs with Lemon Tahini Dressing

Kebab Ingredients

1 lb. lamb (or beef)
4 or 5 cloves of garlic, minced through a garlic press
1/2 teaspoon salt
1/2 teaspoon freshly ground pepper
1/4 cup finely chopped onion
1/4 cup finely chopped parsley
1 teaspoon cumin
1/4 teaspoon allspice
1 egg
1/4 cup plain bread crumbs

Dressing Ingredients

1 cup of sesame tahini sauce (ground sesame paste found in a jar or can)
1/4 cup (4 - 5 tablespoons) fresh squeezed lemon juice
1 medium clove of garlic minced (use a garlic press)
1/2 cup of hot water (amount depends on desired thickness of finished sauce)
Drizzle of olive oil

Kebab Directions

1. Mix all ingredients very well in a large bowl and chill in the refrigerator for at least an hour, or up to overnight.
2. Form into 20 individual "logs" and skewer on the bamboo skewers.
3. Grill to desired doneness, turning as needed.
4. Drizzle with homemade Lemon Tahini Dressing.

Dressing Directions

1. Place tahini, lemon juice and garlic in a blender or food processor and combine or you can vigorously whisk by hand.
2. Slowly pour in the hot water to desired consistency. The ingredients will come together the more you blend/whisk to combine. Add a light drizzle of olive oil.

Tips

• You will need 20 Bamboo skewers, soaked in water for at least 20 minutes.
• Serve Kufta Kebabs with a simple salad with a sprinkle of feta cheese, kalamata olives and warm pita bread.
• Dressing can be stored in the refrigerator, let it come to room temperature before using. Add a bit of hot water and/or olive oil if it is too thick.

Recipe provided by Mimi Ahmed Knittle

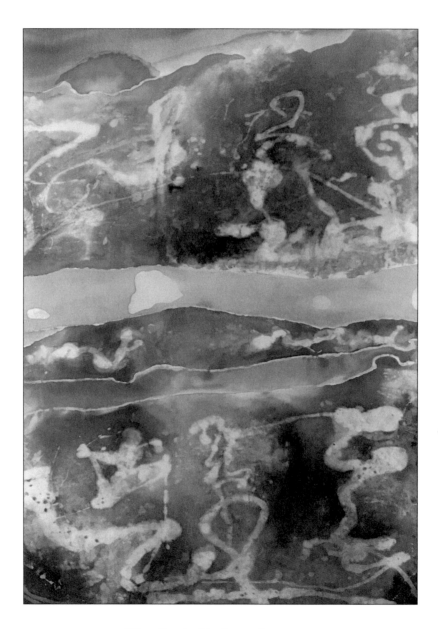

"Blue Granite" by Susan Quateman

Nut Roast

Ingredients

Medium-sized onion
1 oz. butter or margarine
Mushrooms, diced
8 oz. mixed nuts
8 oz. whole meal bread
5 oz. vegetable stock

5 oz. red wine
2 teaspoons Marmite (yeast extract)
1 teaspoon mixed herbs
Salt and pepper to taste
Breadcrumbs
Fried onion rings, optional

Directions

1. Chop onion and sauté in the butter until transparent. Add mushrooms and cook another few minutes.
2. Grind the nuts and bread together in a blender or coffee grinder until quite fine.
3. Heat the stock, wine and yeast extract to the boiling point.
4. Combine all the ingredients together in a bowl and mix well – the mixture should be fairly thick.
5. Turn into a greased, shallow baking dish, level the surface, sprinkle with a few breadcrumbs and bake in the oven at 350 degrees for 30 minutes, until golden brown.
6. Garnish with fried onion rings, if desired.

Tips

• This recipe has many variations. For rissoles – shape the mixture into 6 round cakes. Coat with breadcrumbs and fry until golden brown.
• For a cottage pie alternative – add more liquid to give a loose mixture, spoon into a dish and cover with mashed potato.
• For nut loaf with a cheese and tomato layer – follow the basic recipe for nut roast, but only add 3 - 4 tablespoons of stock/wine to give a firm mixture. Press half the mixture into a greased, 1 lb. loaf tin. Cover with 2 sliced tomatoes and 2 oz. of grated cheese and top with the remaining mixture. Bake as for nut roast. Leave to cool in the tin and then remove carefully. Wrap in plastic wrap or wax paper and put in the refrigerator. Cut into slices for serving.

Recipe provided by Xhazzie Kindle
An adaptation of a recipe from Cranks Restaurant in London.

"At the Trough" by Paul McMahon

Pork Tenderloin Medallions Marsala

Ingredients

Small pork tenderloin
White sauce ingredients – in amount to allow a depth to cover the pork medallions
    2 tablespoons melted butter
    Flour
    Equal parts of milk and Marsala wine (I've also used Madeira or port. Dessert wines work.)
1/2 teaspoon ground or finely chopped rosemary
1/2 teaspoon ground or finely chopped thyme
3/4 teaspoon finely chopped parsley
Salt and pepper

Directions

1. Remove fat and "silver-skin," then slice quarter-inch or slightly less thickness of medallions (a larger slice at the tapered end) from the tenderloin and flatten them with something which has a flat surface. I slam it with the side of a cleaver.
2. Prepare the "white" sauce by gradually adding some of the flour to the butter over low heat. Whisk in a small amount of milk and an equally small amount of the wine. Continue this process until the slightly thick sauce is deep enough to accommodate the medallions in a small or medium frying pan. Mix in the spices and add salt and pepper to taste.
3. Add the pork medallions and heat them at the lowest flame, to preserve tenderness, until they lose redness. A cover will speed the process. Serve warm. Serves 4 - 6.

Tip

• This recipe uses the small tenderloin, which is separated from pork chops when they are made boneless (leaving the tougher side of the chop).

Recipe provided by Don Tritschler

"Festival Waters" by Robin Taliesin

Salmon with Sesame Butter

Ingredients

For Sesame Butter: (Note: This makes enough butter for 8 people)
8 tablespoons unsalted butter (I use regular)
2 tablespoons toasted sesame seeds
2 tablespoons minced chives or scallions
2 teaspoons sesame oil
2 teaspoons soy sauce
Fresh black pepper to taste

For Marinade:
2 tablespoons lime juice
1 tablespoon vegetable oil
1 tablespoon soy sauce

Salmon filet - enough for 4 (8 oz. each)
1 tablespoon sesame seeds
1/2 teaspoon celery seeds

Directions

1. *For Sesame Butter:* Soften butter and stir all ingredients together. Put butter on waxed paper and shape into cylinder about 1-1/4" in diameter. Chill until firm.
2. *For Marinade and Salmon:* Marinate salmon for about 1 hour. Preheat oven to 350 degrees. Toast all celery and sesame seeds; watch so they do not burn. Set aside.
3. Put salmon on baking sheet and bake about 15 - 18 minutes. Do not overcook.
4. Cut filet into serving sizes. Top with 1 or 2 slices of sesame butter (1/4 inch thick). Then sprinkle with 1 tablespoon of sesame seeds and the celery seeds.

Tip
• Toast the seeds for butter and salmon at the same time.

Recipe provided by Ann Welch

"Shrimp" by Diane Bragdon

Shrimp Scampi with Vegetables

Ingredients
1-1/2 sticks butter (Yes!)
2 red peppers, in 2" strips
3/4 lb. zucchini, in 1/2" rounds
3/4 cup chopped shallots
1/4 (or less) cup chopped garlic
1/4 cup drained capers
2 lbs. large shrimp, cleaned & uncooked
1/3 cup chopped basil
Rice, cooked

Directions
1. Melt butter and saute red peppers, zucchini, shallots and garlic for about 4 minutes until soft; do not overcook vegetables. Add capers. Put in baking dish. (Note: You may do this ahead to this point.)
2. Preheat oven to 450 degrees. Stir in raw shrimp. Bake for 15 - 20 minutes, stirring occasionally.
3. Add chopped basil just before serving over rice. Serves 6.

Recipe provided by Ann Welch

"Good painting is like good cooking; it can be tasted, but not explained."

~Maurice de Vlaminck

"The Landing" by Paul McMahon

Sole & Brie

Ingredients
2 filets of Dover Sole (flounder is good, too)
1 wedge of brie
Cilantro (or parsley), chopped
1 cup of chardonnay (or riesling)

Directions
1. Coat the bottom and sides of a casserole dish with butter.
2. Shave the rind off the brie and slice it into 1/4" chunks.
3. Cut strips of fish wide enough to match the thickness of the brie and long enough to wrap around the chunks of brie.
4. Place the fish/brie, end up and together, into the casserole dish.
5. Scatter the cilantro on the fish and pour the wine over it all until it reaches the top of the fish.
6. Heat the oven to 425 degrees; bake uncovered for 8 minutes. Serves 2.

Tip
• This recipe is easily doubled or tripled.

Recipe provided by Don Tritschler
I learned this recipe while biking with the Top of the Hill Gang from a barge in Holland. Our good fortune was to be on the barge owned by a former Holland-America Line chef. His cooking was indeed tasty.

"He was a bold man that first ate an oyster."
~ Jonathan Swift

"Top o' the Morning" by Sheila Farren Billings

Tiled Cottage Pie

Ingredients

2 tablespoons vegetable oil

1 medium onion, finely chopped

2 medium carrots, finely chopped

2 stalks celery, finely chopped

Salt and pepper, to taste

1-1/2 - 2 lbs. meatloaf mix or variation
    of (ground beef, pork, lamb, veal)

3 tablespoons flour

2 teaspoons Worcestershire sauce

1-1/2 cups chicken or beef stock

4 sprigs fresh thyme

1-1/2 cups frozen peas, rinsed in colander

3 baking (russet) potatoes, sliced
    very thin and in a bowl of water

1 tablespoon butter cut into small pieces

Butter

1/2 cup shredded sharp cheese

Directions

1. Set oven to 375 degrees. Butter a 9" square baking dish, or something similar. In a large skillet over medium heat, heat the oil. Add the onions, carrots and celery, salt and pepper and cook, stirring often for 10 minutes.

2. Add the meat mixture and cook, stirring often for 5 minutes or until brown. Move meat to one side of pan and spoon off excess fat. Stir in the flour, cook and stir for 2 minutes. Add Worcestershire sauce and stock, turn down heat to medium-high and stir until mixture comes to a boil. Let bubble for 3 minutes.

3. Remove the pan from heat. Stir in thyme and peas. Taste for seasoning and add more salt and pepper if needed. Transfer mixture to baking dish.

4. Drain potato slices and dry with a paper towel. Arrange the slices in rows, overlapping so it creates a tiled effect. Dot with the butter and sprinkle with cheese.

5. Bake pie for 50 - 60 minutes. Check to be sure potatoes are cooked through with a fork and the top is brown and bubbling around the edges. Let it sit for 5 minutes, then cut and serve. Serves 4. Enjoy!

Recipe provided by Missy Fisher
This is such a yummy dish for a laid-back evening with good friends.
Serve with a salad and it's completely satisfying.

Chocolate comes from cocoa, which is a tree, that makes it a plant. Chocolate is salad!

~Unknown

Sweets & Baked Treats

"The Green Pitcher" by Heather Johnson Reid

Apple Crisp

Ingredients

2 cups almond flour
1/2 teaspoon sea salt
1 tablespoon cinnamon
1/2 teaspoon nutmeg
1/2 cup grapeseed oil (can use canola)
1/2 cup pure maple syrup
1 tablespoon vanilla extract
5 medium apples, peeled, sliced and chopped

Directions

1. Combine almond flour, salt, cinnamon and nutmeg.
2. In another bowl, combine oil, maple syrup and vanilla.
3. Stir wet ingredients into dry.
4. Place apples in a glass baking dish and spoon topping over them.
5. Cover loosely with foil and bake at 350 degrees for 50 minutes.
6. When apples are soft and bubbly, remove foil and bake 10 minutes more to brown the top. Good served warm or at room temperature.

Tip

• Can use any fruit in season, great with peaches, blueberries, pears, etc.

Recipe provided by Jill Hamilton

"Life is uncertain. Eat dessert first."

~Ernestine Ulmer

"Plate of Cookies" by Claudia Kaufman

Beacon Hill Cookies

Ingredients

12 oz. semi-sweet chocolate chips
4 egg whites
Dash of salt twice
1 cup sugar
1 teaspoon vanilla
1 teaspoon apple cider vinegar
3/4 cup chopped walnuts

Directions

1. Melt chocolate chips over hot water in double boiler or saucepan in water.
2. Beat egg whites with salt until foamy. Gradually add sugar, beating well, until stiff peaks form.
3. Beat in vanilla and vinegar.
4. Fold in melted chocolate and walnuts.
5. Drop by teaspoonfuls on greased cookie sheet.
6. Bake at 325 degrees for approximately 10 minutes.

Recipe provided by Karen McMahon

"A balanced diet is a cookie in each hand."

~Barbara Johnson

"Bowl of Blueberries" by Claudia Kaufman

Blueberry Buckle

Ingredients

For Cake:
1/2 cup butter, softened
3/4 cup sugar
1 egg, beaten
2 cups flour
2-1/2 teaspoons baking powder
1/4 teaspoon salt
1/2 cup milk
2 cups fresh blueberries

For Crumb Topping:
1/2 cup sugar
1/2 cup flour
1/2 teaspoon cinnamon
1/4 cup butter, softened

Directions

1. Cream butter and sugar together.
2. Add egg and mix well.
3. Sift flour, baking powder and salt together.
4. Add to creamed mixture alternating with the milk.
5. Spread in a greased pan. Either a 9" square or 12 x 8" rectangular pan works.
6. Sprinkle blueberries over the batter.
7. Combine all four topping ingredients together until crumbly. Sprinkle over the blueberries.
8. Bake at 350 degrees for 45 - 50 minutes. Buon Appetito!

Recipe provided by Christine Nuccio

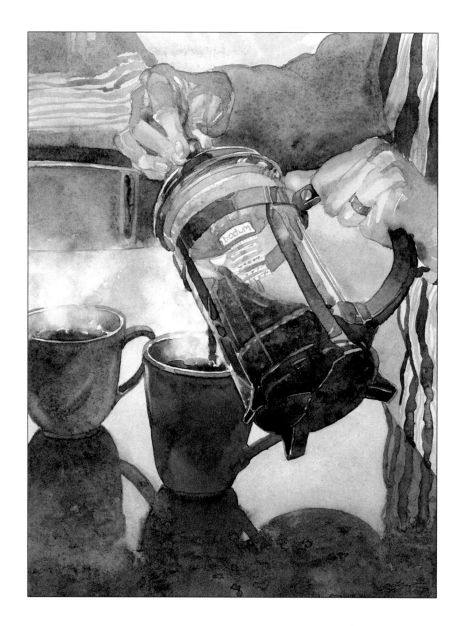

"Pre-caffeinated" by Frank Costantino

Breakfast Bread Pudding with Warm Berry Sauce

Ingredients

For Bread Pudding:
2 eggs
3/4 cup granulated sugar
3 cups low fat milk
1 cup heavy cream
1/2 cup unsalted butter, melted
1 tablespoon vanilla extract
3/4 cup raisins
1 teaspoon freshly grated nutmeg
8 oz. stale French bread, sliced 1/2" thick

For Warm Berry Sauce:
2 cups fresh or frozen raspberries
2 cups fresh or frozen strawberries
1/3 cup sugar
1/3 cup freshly squeezed orange juice
3 tablespoons fresh lemon juice
Powdered sugar for dusting
Whole fresh raspberries & strawberries,
   for garnish

Directions

1. *For the Bread Pudding:* Combine the eggs, sugar, milk, cream, melted butter, vanilla, raisins, and nutmeg in a bowl; whisk to blend well.
2. Pour the mixture over the bread slices in a large bowl and let stand, turning bread as necessary, until bread is soft and saturated, about 20 minutes.
3. Preheat the oven to 350 degrees. Arrange the bread slices in a lightly greased 4 quart baking dish and pour any unabsorbed custard mixture over the bread. Bake uncovered until the custard is set and the top is lightly browned, about 45 minutes.
4. *For the Warm Berry Sauce:* Combine the berries, sugar, orange juice, lemon juice, in a saucepan over medium heat. Cook, stirring continuously, until the fruit begins to break up, about 5 minutes.
5. Puree in a food processor or blender. This can be made ahead and warmed up for serving.
6. To serve, dust the top of the pudding with powdered sugar. Pass the warm sauce and berries at the table. Serves 8.

Recipe provided by Karen McMahon
This is WAY easier than it sounds!! It's delicious, and a great brunch treat!

"If You Have Any Questions" by Janet Albert

Chocolate Pots de Crème

Ingredients

2/3 cup sugar
2 tablespoons cornstarch
1/8 teaspoon kosher salt
3 cups whole milk
4 large egg yolks
1/2 teaspoon vanilla extract
6 oz. top quality bittersweet chocolate, chopped
Optional: unsweetened cocoa powder and fresh whipped cream

Directions

1. Mix together the sugar, cornstarch and salt in a medium saucepan. Add 1/3 cup of the milk, stirring to form a smooth paste. Whisk in the remaining milk and the egg yolks.
2. Cook the pudding mixture over medium-low heat, stirring constantly with a wooden spoon or spatula until thickened, about 15 minutes. Do not allow it to boil.
3. Remove from heat. Add the vanilla and chocolate, stirring until the chocolate is melted and the mixture is smooth.
4. Pour into eight 4 oz. ramekins, glasses or teacups and refrigerate until well chilled, at least 2 hours and up to 48 hours.
5. Sprinkle with the cocoa powder and/or serve with fresh whipped cream. Serves 8.

Tips

• Hands on time: 30 minutes.
• Total time: 2-1/2 hours including chilling.

Recipe provided by Missy Fisher

"Vortex" by Robin Taliesin

Dutch Chocolate Pudding

Ingredients
1 envelope plain gelatin
Sugar, to taste, or Stevia
3 tablespoons of unsweetened cocoa
2 cups of milk (reconstituted is okay)
1 teaspoon of vanilla

Directions
1. In saucepan, mix gelatin, sweetener and cocoa.
2. Add milk and heat to just boiling.
3. Add vanilla.
4. Pour into custard dishes, chill until firm. Serves 4 - 6, depending on size of dessert dishes.

Recipe provided by Diana Hosley Burchfield

"Food is symbolic of love when words are inadequate."
~Alan D. Wolfelt

"Pitcher & Lemons" by Sheila Farren Billings

Four-Layer Lemon Torte with Lemon Cream Cheese Frosting

Ingredients

For Cake:

1 yellow cake mix (or lemon)
1/2 cup butter, room temperature
6 large eggs
1/2 cup whipping cream
1/2 cup water
1 tablespoon grated lemon peel

For Frosting:

(3) 8 oz. packages cream cheese, room temperature
(1) 11 oz. jar of lemon curd
1 cup sugar
2 tablespoons lemon juice
1 tablespoon grated lemon peel
3/4 cup raspberry preserves (optional)
1-1/2 cups sliced almonds, toasted (optional)

Directions

1. Preheat oven to 350 degrees. Butter 2 springform pans.
2. Combine first 6 ingredients for cake. Beat 2 minutes. Divide batter into pans. Bake until tester comes out clean, about 28 minutes. Cool completely.
3. Beat cream cheese and curd for frosting. Add sugar, lemon juice and peel. Beat well. (This makes more frosting than required. Could almost cut by 1/3).
4. When cool, cut each cake in half horizontally. Place 1 slice cut side up on platter. Spread with 1/4 jam, then 3/4 cup frosting.
5. Repeat with all layers BUT put last cake on top with the smooth side up.
6. Frost top and sides of cake. Press almonds onto sides of cake.
7. Chill until cake sets, 2 hours.

Recipe provided by Ann Welch

"Dessert Banquet" by Marjorie Rizzo

Grandma's Chocolate Cake
with Whipped Cream Frosting

Ingredients

For Cake:

1-3/4 cups flour

2 cups sugar

3/4 cup cocoa

2 teaspoons baking soda

1 teaspoon baking powder

1 teaspoon salt

2 eggs

1 cup strong black coffee (can be substituted with 2 teaspoons instant in 1 cup boiling water)

1 cup buttermilk

1/2 cup vegetable oil

1 teaspoon vanilla

For Frosting:

I pint of whipping cream

1 teaspoon of vanilla

1 teaspoon of sugar

Directions

1. Combine flour, cocoa, baking soda, baking powder and salt in a large bowl.
2. Add eggs, coffee, buttermilk, vegetable oil and vanilla.
3. Beat for 2 minutes on medium speed.
4. Bake at 350 degrees for 30 - 35 minutes.
5. For frosting, combine ingredients and beat until stiff.

Tip

• If you would like you can add cocoa powder to taste for a chocolate frosting.

Recipe provided by Patti Baker

"Fruit Cup" by Claudia Kaufman

Lexa's Blueberry & Peach Cobbler

Ingredients

For Filling:
1 pint blueberries
2 cups sliced peaches
1 tablespoon lemon juice
1/2 cup sugar
1/4 cup flour
1/2 teaspoon cinnamon
1/4 teaspoon cloves

For Topping:
3/4 cup sifted flour
1/3 cup rolled oats
1/2 cup light brown sugar
1/3 cup melted butter or margarine

Directions

1. Preheat oven to 375 degrees.
2. Mix filling ingredients and put in 8 x 8" pan.
3. Add topping.
4. Bake for 35 minutes. Serves 4 - 6.

Tip

• Excellent served warm with vanilla ice cream.

Recipe provided by Ann Welch

"Oranges & Mangoes on Table" by Frank Costantino

Orange Fruit Cake

Ingredients

The rind and juice from one orange

1 cup raisins

1/2 cup pecans

1/2 cup butter

1 cup granulated sugar

1 teaspoon vanilla

2 eggs

2 cups flour

1 teaspoon baking soda

2/3 cup buttermilk

Directions

1. Preheat oven to 325 degrees.
2. Put orange rind, raisins and pecans into a food processor. Pulse until finely chopped.
3. In a separate bowl using a stand mixer or a hand mixer, cream butter, add sugar, vanilla then eggs. Beat well until combined.
4. Sift together dry ingredients (flour and baking soda) and add to butter mixture alternating with the buttermilk. Mix until combined.
5. Fold in the orange, raisin and pecan mixture.
6. Turn into a buttered (or sprayed) tube pan.
7. Bake for 1 hour at 325 degrees.
8. For glaze: In a small bowl, squeeze the juice of the orange that you used for the rind and add 1/2 cup of granulated sugar. Stir well until dissolved. Pour glaze over the cake while still very warm.

Recipe provided by Mimi Ahmed Knittle

This moist and delicious cake recipe is from my Grandmother Van Houtte and has always been a family favorite for birthdays and holidays. It was a time consuming process when she made it using a hand food grinder. Now we can make it with much less effort (but no less love!) using a food processor.

"Apple Pair" by Mimi Ahmed Knittle

Pennsylvania Dutch Apple Dumplings

Ingredients

6 apples, peeled and cored (McIntosh, Gala,
    Honeycrisp or your favorite baking apple)

For the dough:
2 cups all purpose flour
2-1/2 teaspoons baking powder
1/2 teaspoon salt
2/3 cup softened butter
1/2 cup milk

Filling for inside the cored apple:
2 teaspoons cinnamon
3 teaspoons granulated sugar

For the brown sugar cinnamon syrup:
2 cups brown sugar
2 cups water
1/4 cup butter
1/2 teaspoon cinnamon

Directions

1. In a medium size bowl, combine the flour, baking powder and salt.
2. Mix in the butter, add milk and mix just until a soft dough forms.
3. Divide the dough into six equal balls. On a floured surface, roll each ball into a circle (keeping each circle roughly even in diameter and thickness).
4. Place a peeled and cored apple in the center of each dough circle.
5. Sprinkle a teaspoon full of cinnamon sugar mixture into the center of each cored apple.
6. Fold the dough up around the apple, pressing the edges and sealing the top.
7. Coat a 9 x 13" Pyrex or other baking pan with butter or cooking spray.
8. In a small saucepan, combine the brown sugar, water, butter and cinnamon over medium to low heat. Heat until just simmering, watching and stirring often.
9. Place the dough covered apples in the pan and pour the brown sugar cinnamon mixture over the dumplings. Optional: brush dumpling with egg wash and sprinkle with granulated sugar.
10. Bake at 350 degrees for 30 minutes until the apples are soft and the dough is a golden brown color. Serve warm with sauce spooned over the dumpling.

Tip

• These apples are wrapped in a soft homemade dough and baked in a cinnamon brown sugar syrup. Best if eaten warm with a little vanilla ice cream and the warm syrup spooned over the top.

Recipe provided by Mimi Ahmed Knittle

"Pumpkins" by Barbara Naeser

Pumpkin Bars

Ingredients

1/2 cup pumpkin puree (can use butternut or other squash)
1/2 cup pure maple syrup
2 eggs
1 cup almond flour
1/4 teaspoon sea salt
1/2 teaspoon baking soda
1/4 teaspoon cinnamon
1/4 teaspoon nutmeg
1/4 teaspoon cloves

Directions

1. Combine pumpkin, maple syrup and eggs.
2. Add dry ingredients until well combined.
3. Pour batter into a greased and floured 8 x 8" baking dish.
4. Bake at 350 degrees for 35 minutes. Delicious!

Recipe provided by Jill Hamilton

"A party without cake is just a meeting."

~Julia Child

"Lemonade Stand" by Sheila Farren Billings

Refrigerator Cookies

Ingredients

1 cup butter
2 cups sugar
2 eggs
3-1/2 cups flour
4 teaspoons baking powder
1 teaspoon vanilla
1 teaspoon salt

Directions

1. Preheat oven to 425 degrees.
2. Combine all ingredients until a dough forms.
3. Roll dough into a log, wrap in plastic wrap and chill in the refrigerator.
4. After dough has chilled, slice into circles and place each on a lightly greased cookie sheet.
5. Decorate before baking with a pinch of granulated sugar or "jimmies" or "sprinkles."
6. Bake until edges are slightly browned.

Recipe provided by Barbara Rafferty
A hundred-year-old family recipe.

"Cookies are made of butter and love."

~Norwegian Proverb

"Chocolate-Dipped Strawberries" by Claudia Kaufman

Rich Vegan Chocolate Cake

Ingredients

For Cake:
1-3/4 cups whole wheat flour
  (can substitute gluten free flour)
2 teaspoons baking powder
1 teaspoon baking soda
1/2 teaspoon sea salt
1 cup milk (almond, soy or rice, can also
  use regular milk, if you're not vegan)
3/4 cup good cocoa powder (without sugar)
1/2 cup canola or grapeseed oil
1-1/2 cups pure maple syrup
1 teaspoon apple cider vinegar
2 teaspoons vanilla

For Frosting:
3 oz. unsweetened baking chocolate
1/3 cup milk (whatever kind you would
  like to use)
1/2 cup pure maple syrup
1 teaspoon vanilla

Directions

1. Spray a 9" springform pan with nonstick cooking spray and dust with flour and line with parchment.
2. Sift flour, baking powder, baking soda and salt together.
3. Heat milk on medium-low heat and add cocoa powder. Whisk until it is dissolved.
4. Combine other liquid ingredients in a bowl and whisk well.
5. Add cocoa mixture and combine.
6. Add wet ingredients to the dry.
7. Pour batter into prepared pan and bake at 350 degrees for 25 minutes or until a toothpick comes out clean. Let cool and frost.
8. *For Frosting:* Melt chocolate in milk over low heat.
9. Remove from heat and mix in maple syrup and vanilla. Let cool, will be liquidy. Spread on top of cake and refrigerate to let it set up a bit before serving.

Recipe provided by Jill Hamilton
Sinfully delicious, even if you are not vegan.

"Farm Fresh Eggs" by Elaine Abrams

Walnut Dreams

Ingredients

1 cup butter
1/2 cup sugar
2 cups all purpose flour
1 lb. brown sugar
2 cups chopped walnuts
1/4 cup flour
4 eggs
1 teaspoon salt
1 teaspoon baking powder
1 teaspoon vanilla

For Frosting: (Optional, I never do this, they are already rich)
2 cups powdered sugar
3 tablespoons milk
2 tablespoons butter, melted
Almond extract

Directions

(1/2 of this will do easily)

1. Preheat oven to 350 degrees. Grease 12 x 18" (or a bit smaller) jelly roll pan.
2. Cream 1 cup butter with 1/2 cup sugar. Gradually add flour. (I use a food processor, don't over mix).
3. Spread evenly in pan. It will seem very thin but it's okay. Bake for 15 minutes.
4. Combine next 7 ingredients and blend well. Pour over crust. Continue baking until set, about 15 - 17 minutes (or more). Let cool completely.
5. Frost if desired. Cut into squares or diamonds.

Tip

• Increasing the crust by almost 50% works well, too.

Recipe provided by Ann Welch

"Lemon Study" by Charlie Allen

Wendy's Cheesecake

Ingredients

For Filling:
(3) 8 oz. packages of cream cheese
3/4 cup sugar
3 eggs
1 teaspoon vanilla
1/4 cup finely ground lemon rind
1 teaspoon lemon juice
1/2 cup finely grated unsweetened
    coconut (optional)

For Crust:
1 cup+ of Ginger Snaps, Lemon Snaps
    or Graham Crackers, crushed
Coconut oil
Sugar

For Topping:
Fruit of choice, fresh or as a syrup

Directions

1. *For Filling:* In a big bowl, cream the cream cheese with the sugar. In another bowl beat the eggs and mix in well with the cream cheese/sugar mixture, adding vanilla, lemon rind and lemon juice. Also add coconut, if desired.
2. *For Crust:* Use coconut oil to grease an ovenware glass or metal 9" pie pan. Crush cookies mixed with a bit of coconut oil & sugar. Press crumb mixture, about 1/8" thick, onto bottom and side surfaces of pan.
3. Bake in oven at 325 degrees for about an hour, or until knife inserted in the almost set center of filling comes out clean. Do not overcook.
4. *For Topping:* When pie has cooled (may take an hour +), add your favorite fruit, whole, smashed or in a syrup. Also, coconut flakes, if desired. Eat at room temperature or chill and then add fruit.

Tip

• Measurements of sugar, vanilla, lemon juice and coconut are approximate. Adjust to suit your taste by sampling filling before spreading it into the pan.

Recipe provided by Judy Trujillo

"Carrots" by Elaine Abrams

Whole Grain Carrot Cake Loaf

Ingredients

1-1/2 cups grated carrots (or apples or zucchini)
1 egg, beaten (or use 1 tablespoon ground flax seed to make vegan)
1/2 cup pure maple syrup
3/4 cup almond milk minus 2 tablespoons
　　(or other non-dairy milk or other liquid such as apple juice or apple cider)
1/3 cup grapeseed oil (or oil of your choice)
1-1/2 teaspoons vanilla extract
1/2 teaspoon apple cider vinegar
1-1/2 cups whole wheat flour (or gluten free flour)
2 teaspoons ground cinnamon
1/2 teaspoon ground ginger
2 teaspoons baking powder
1/2 teaspoon baking soda
1/4 teaspoon sea salt
1/2 cup raisins, soaked for 10 minutes and drained
1/4 cup walnuts, chopped

Directions

1. Lightly grease loaf pan and flour.
2. Mix together liquid ingredients, egg or flax seed and grated carrot (apple or zucchini).
3. Mix dry ingredients in another bowl.
4. Pour wet ingredients into dry and stir until just combined.
5. Fold in raisins and walnuts.
6. Pour into prepared pan and bake at 350 degrees for 45 minutes or until a toothpick comes out clean.

Tips

• This recipe works equally well if you replace the carrots with apples or zucchini.
• Freezes well.

Recipe provided by Jill Hamilton

"I cook with wine. Sometimes I even add it to the food."

~W.C. Fields

Beverages

"Celestial Blue" by Susan Quateman and Les Bartlett

Blues Brothers Martini

Ingredients
Fresh blueberries
3 oz. Blueberry Stoli vodka
1/2 oz. citrus/basil-infused simple syrup
1/2 oz. fresh lemon juice, plus rind for garnish
Splash of club soda

Directions
1. Place fresh blueberries in a Boston Shaker and muddle.
2. Fill a shaker with ice; add vodka, simple syrup and lemon juice, shake well.
3. Strain into a chilled martini glass; top with a splash of club soda.
4. Garnish with a twist of lemon rind.

Tip
• Add lemon juice and basil leaves to plain simple syrup, heat then let cool and strain.

Recipe provided by Wicks Brick Oven Restaurant
www.warwickplace.com/wicks | 123 Pleasant Street, Marblehead

"Oh, you hate your job? Why didn't you say so? There's a support group for that. It's called EVERYBODY, and they meet at the bar."

~Drew Carey

"Cherry on Top" by Claudia Kaufman

Da Nang Martini

Ingredients
3/4 oz. Tito's vodka
3/4 oz. Aperol
3/4 oz. St. Germaine
3/4 oz. lime juice
1/2 oz. passion fruit syrup

Directions
1. Fill a cocktail shaker with ice.
2. Combine ingredients and shake well.
3. Strain into a chilled martini glass.

Tip
• Passion fruit syrup can be sourced from www.thebostonshaker.com.

As sampled at Tiger Mama Restaurant
www.tigermamaboston.com | 1363 Boylston Street, Boston

"I love to drink martinis. Two at the very most. Three I'm under the table. Four I'm under my host."

~Dorothy Parker

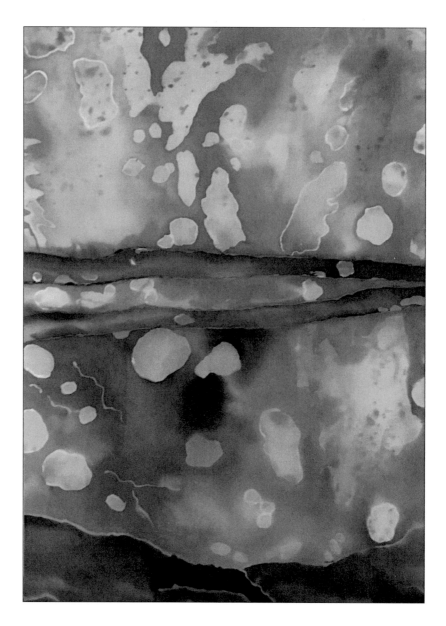

"Golden Granite" by Susan Quateman

Green with Envy Martini

Ingredients

5 cucumber slices
5 - 6 mint leaves
Wedge of lime
2-1/2 oz. Prairie Organic Cucumber vodka
1 oz. St. Elder (or you can use St. Germaine)
1 oz. fresh lime juice
1 oz. simple syrup

Directions

1. Muddle 4 cucumber slices, mint leaves and lime wedge.
2. Place in a cocktail shaker and fill with ice. Add the vodka, St. Elder, lime juice and simple syrup. Shake well.
3. Strain into a frosted martini glass.
4. Garnish with a cucumber slice.

Recipe provided by 5 Corners Kitchen
www.5cornerskitchen.com | 2 School Street, Marblehead

"I drink to make other people more interesting."

~Ernest Hemingway

"Lemon Tree" by Linda Lyons

Lemon Apple Carrot Ginger Juice

Ingredients

2 apples
8 medium carrots
1 lemon
1/2" - 1" piece of ginger (adjust according to preference)

Directions

1. Start with chilled organic produce. Chop all ingredients into 1" pieces and add one at a time to the juicer.
2. Serve over ice with a garnish of green apple or fresh lemon slice. Makes 2 cups.

Recipe provided by Linda Lyons
When life gives one lemons, find some apples, carrots and ginger too.
Sometimes simple recipes really are best. Enjoy this little bit of sunshine in a glass
whenever a quick dose of vitamins and antioxidants are needed. This sweet and spicy
juice also cleanses the digestive system and boosts metabolism. One glass provides
the daily recommended dose of Vitamin A and C, as well as essential
nutrients to maintain good health, skin and vision.

"Jar of Limons" by Claudia Kaufman

Lemon Basil Martini

Ingredients

6 big leaves of fresh basil
1/2 oz. fresh lemon juice
2 oz. St. Germaine
2 oz. Ketel One vodka

Directions

1. Fill a cocktail shaker with ice; tear the basil leaves into small pieces and place in shaker.
2. Add the lemon juice, St. Germaine & vodka. Shake well.
3. Strain into a chilled martini glass.
4. Garnish with a lemon twist.

Recipe provided by Caffé Italia Trattoria & Bar
www.caffeitaliarestaurant.com | 10 School Street, Marblehead

"A man's got to believe in something. I believe I'll have another drink." ~W. C. Fields

"Lichen on a Granite Wall" by Susan Quateman

Moscow Mule Variations

Pomegranate Moscow Mule

Ingredients
2 oz. of pomegranate juice
2 oz. of Pama pomegranate liqueur
2 oz. of vodka (regular or citron,
    to your taste)
One bottle/can of ginger beer
Juice from half a lime, plus slices
Fresh pomegranate seeds

Directions
1. Combine all of the above ingredients.
2. Pour over crushed ice into two copper mugs.
3. Garnish with pomegranate seeds and a lime slice.

Peach Smash Moscow Mule

Ingredients
1/2 oz. of Peach Schnapps
1 oz. of vodka
Splash of Grand Marnier as a topper
1/2 of a ripe peach, diced
Juice from a lime
One bottle/can of ginger beer

Directions
1. Using a large cocktail shaker, muddle a few lime wedges and the diced ripe peach.
2. Add Peach Schnapps, crushed ice and the vodka. Shake and let chill for a minute.
3. Pour contents into a tall clear glass. Add ice if needed. Fill glass with the ginger beer and top with a splash of Grand Marnier.
4. Garnish with a lime slice and a festive straw.

Tips
• Moscow Mules are a popular drink. Traditionally served in a chilled copper mug, this cocktail's presentation is as enticing as the drink itself.
• The traditional Moscow Mule is made with just the vodka, ginger beer and lime juice. If you substitute rum for the vodka, it becomes a popular sailor's choice, the Dark and Stormy. Substitute the vodka with bourbon and it is called a Kentucky Mule.

Recipes provided by Mimi Ahmed Knittle

"A Pair" by Marie Sweeney

The Humphrey Cocktail

Ingredients
Equal parts:
Pear vodka
Cranberry juice
Fresh lime juice
Pear juice or nectar
Sage simple syrup

Directions
1. Pour all ingredients into shaker full of ice.
2. Shake vigorously and strain into martini glass.
3. Rub rim of glass with fresh sage leaf then float on top.

Recipe provided by Turtle Cove Bar & Grille
www.turtlecovebarandgrille.com | 165 Pleasant Street, Marblehead

*History of 'The Humphrey' – Marblehead residents and Chef/Owner's Gayle
and Stephane Colinet named this drink after the town turkey turned town mascot
that many locals called 'Humphrey' as he was often seen meandering on that street.
Some saw Humphrey's street walking as a nuisance while others took it as a sign to
slow down and smile. With the passing of this feathered icon, it was decided that
'The Humphrey' shall forever remain on Turtle Cove's cocktail menu!*

"Landing Pub" by Kristen Nyberg

The Sailaway Martini

Ingredients

2 oz. Nautical gin
1/2 oz. simple syrup
1 oz. Lemon juice
Champagne

Directions

1. Pour first three ingredients into shaker full of ice and mix.
2. Pour into a martini glass and top with champagne.
3. Serve straight up.

Recipe provided by The Landing Restaurant, Deck & Pub
www.thelandingrestaurant.com | 81 Front Street, Marblehead

"Of all the gin joints in all the towns in all the world, she walks into mine."

~Rick Blaine; Played by Humphrey Bogart in the film "Casablanca"

"Afternoon Tipple" by Susan Schrader

Made in the USA
Middletown, DE
29 June 2017